I0414255

A Case Against Alcohol Prohibition In India

Copyright 2014 Sukant Khurana and Brooks G. Robinson
First published as Ebook by Sukant Khurana and Brooks G. Robinson at Smashwords

Printed in 2016 by Create Space as paperback book.

Table of Contents

Acknowledgements

This book is amalgamation of our writings over last few years. We are thankful to websites that have published our articles and enabled informed discourse on alcohol related issues in India. We have only credited the websites in our list of references that first published our select articles but some posts have been shared by several other sources. We could not list them all but we are thankful to everyone who have shared and enjoyed our writings. We are thankful to our loved ones for their support during writing of this book. We are also thankful to several people who have provided constructive criticism over the years on our scientific research, popular science writings and policy suggestions. While this book is not about our neuroscience research but without the initial encouragement of senior neuroscience colleagues at the University of Texas at Austin, specifically Prof. Robert Adron Harris, Prof. Richard Aldrich, Prof. Nigel Atkinson and Dr. Morikawa, we might not have pursued addiction research. We are thankful to them as we are to our friends Dr. Alfredo Ghezzi, Dr. Luisa Scott, Wen-ke Li and late Dr. Jascha Pohl for several intellectually stimulating conversations. We also benefitted tremendously during our respective stay at Austin from our interaction with Prof. Harold Zakon, Prof. Daniel Johnston, and Dr. Nace Golding on neuroscience research. Our biological research drove our interest into the societal side of addiction to be able to deal with the problem holistically from all ends. Sukant Khurana designed the cover art.

References

This book is amalgamation of few of our select works. Here is the list of the original works that have been the source material for this book.

1. Symptoms of alcohol poisoning by tainted hooch. Robinson and Khurana. December 18, 2011 http://www.kvartha.com/

2. Can We Stop The Carnage Of Illicit Hooch Through Information And Timely Medical Intervention? Robinson and Khurana. December 27 2011 http://www.scoop.co.nz/

3. Fear Of Police Killed Many In Hooch Tragedy. December 19 2011. Countercurrents.org

4. 150 People Died After Drinking Tainted Alcohol: Can One Survive After Drinking Tainted Hooch? Robinson and Khurana December 25, 2011, http://www.youthkiawaaz.com/

5. Debunking Myths About Alcohol. Khurana and Robinson. May 2 2013 http://www.youthkiawaaz.com/

6. Enjoy Festive Season With Moderation In Drinking. Debunking Popular Alcohol Related Fads And Fiction. Robinson and Khurana. 27 December 2011 http://www.scoop.co.nz/

7. Make an informed choice about alcohol consumption. Khurana and Robinson. April 30, 2011 http://www.dailytexanonline.com/

8. The Ban On Alcohol Advertisements Is Futile As Long As This Hypocrisy Exists. Khurana. August 22, 2011, http://www.youthkiawaaz.com/

9. Gujarat: a disaster case study for amending alcohol policies in India. Khurana. December 29, 2013 http://www.theworldreporter.com

10. The Root Causes of Alcoholism in India; Possible Solutions. Khurana. August 11, 2011 http://www.theworldreporter.com

11. The Need To Tackle The Good, Bad And Ugly Of Alcohol Consumption. Khurana. December 26, 2013

Prologue

Alcohol is usually good in moderation and bad in excess. It is a mixed blessing, except for a small section of population that becomes dependent on it, for which it is only a curse. Alcohol addiction can be devastating to the addicts and their families. A knee-jerk solution of complete prohibition has been tried in various parts of the world to solve the problem of addiction but without much success. Alcohol use, abuse and regulation are all nuanced issues that require evidence-based dynamic policymaking. Unfortunately alcohol regulation has become highly politicized, with the interference of religious influences in a constitutionally secular India becoming an ever-growing trend. Despite there being plenty of examples of disasters of kneejerk alcohol regulation policies, such as the infamous US prohibition, India has been repeating several mistakes of the West. With such concerns in mind, we have compiled, restructured and edited our previous popular newspaper and magazine writings on alcohol issues that are germane to the situation. The points we make are fairly general and the book is not a work of on ground research but a review of overall status of the situation. None of the arguments in the book should be taken as medical advice. The goal of this book is to initiate a dialogue for smarter alcohol usage and regulation in India.

Chapter 1
Myths surrounding alcohol

India is a country of increasing alcohol consumption but there are many myths that surround alcohol and alcoholism in India. While for those who do not drink, the safest advise is to avoid drinking but what is not safe at all is for the Indian population to have an oversimplified black and white picture of alcohol consumption. For those who enjoy a drink or two, there are healthy alcohol drinking habits and if myths around alcohol are removed we can have more responsible alcohol consumption in India.

MYTH: Alcohol is always bad

Many view alcohol as a pure evil that can't do any good. It can cause more harm than good, but the effects of alcohol are a function of the amount of alcohol consumed, by the age and health status of the individual, place, the company, the time of the day and the activities partaken after drinking. Alcohol consumption comes with both positive and negative health consequences. In large, highly intoxicating doses, alcohol is almost always negative. It depresses the human central nervous system causing effects ranging from a reduction in reaction time to alterations in spatial judgment and even fatality with a high enough dose. Regular consumption of a large amount of alcohol damages vital organs such as the liver and kidney. Alcoholics develop a dependency on alcohol to the point that they cannot function in its absence, and can even experience epileptic seizures when alcohol is abruptly withdrawn. Even small amounts can be highly dangerous for people with a liver infection or disease, or people taking depression medications or those that cause an increased level of sedation.

However, in small doses, alcohol can be beneficial to a healthy adult. Alcohol can act as a social lubricant and bond people in long-lasting friendships. Regular consumption of low but not high, amounts of alcohol can also have many health benefits. Low amounts of alcohol, one to three drinks of alcohol a day, have been correlated with reduced dementia and Alzheimer's disease, improved cardiac functioning, and reduced stroke incidences, type 2 diabetes, osteoporosis, gallbladder diseases, arthritis, renal cell carcinoma, thyroid cancer, and non-Hodgkin lymphoma. If one does not drink, these possible mild benefits should not encourage someone to start drinking, as correlation should not be confused with causation. All this extensive literature shows convincingly is that in mild amounts there are likely not significant health consequences for healthy subjects. Pregnant women should avoid alcohol altogether because regular consumption of high amounts of alcohol can result in fetal alcohol syndrome in the unborn child. For some women, even small doses of ethanol can be damaging to the fetus. People with liver problems and those taking certain antidepressants should also stay away from alcohol altogether. Those who do not drink alcohol should stay away from it because the dangers of excess far outweigh the benefits of moderation. The same health benefits can be accessed from many other food sources and regular exercise. Those who do consume alcohol, however, should pick up healthy habits of moderate drinking and avoid excessive consumption.

MYTH: Alcohol makes people happier

While the initial effects of alcohol can include euphoria and hyper-excitation, alcohol in higher amounts is actually a numbing influence. The depressant effects of alcohol can manifest as sleepiness or lethargy, an inability to comprehend situations, altered judgments and mood changes. Interestingly, alcohol affects everyone somewhat differently. Some people become very sad and withdrawn, while others become more jovial. It is good to know how the drug affects you so you do not end up regretting a drinking session. In a recent scientific study, risk-prone individuals lost their fear of negative consequences when they consumed alcohol, whereas alcohol did not elicit any change in a group that was averse to risk. Alcohol only makes people happy because of creating social bonds and friendship. This is only possible when people are not drunk out of their senses but enjoying mild amounts of alcohol.

MYTH: Alcohol is not a serious drug

Alcohol is one of the most widely abused substances in the world. It is highly addictive and it is often more readily available than other narcotics. It can cause devastating health maladies and estrange people from their families and friends. Alcohol also causes a vast number of deaths each year. Apart from aggravating health conditions and directly causing hundreds of thousands of deaths, excessive drinking indirectly impacts society by breaking up poor families and increasing incarceration. If excessive drinking is not serious, we are not sure what is.

MYTH: Alcohol makes sex better

Alcohol lowers people's inhibitions and often makes people feel more comfortable in social situations. This makes approaching strangers and engaging in sexual behaviors more likely for drunken individuals, but alcohol most definitely does not make sex more pleasurable. In fact, alcohol dims sensation, which does not improve sex. It can also prevent men from getting or maintaining an erection and even from ejaculating. In addition, it can decrease the female sex drive. Given the resulting lack of inhibitions and the impairment of judgment, alcohol has been implicated in a significant decrease in the use of condoms and other safe sex practices. The influence of alcohol in the spread of AIDS is a burning research topic with many studies implicating drunken actions responsible for an increase in the spread of the disease.

MYTH: My family has alcohol problems, but I won't get addicted because I know how to handle my drinks

Increased vulnerability for addiction has a strong genetic component and is passed from parents to their kids through both genetic and cultural ways. Cultural factors can also strongly influence many of our behaviors, for example, domestic violence also runs in families. If any of your family members have addiction issues, it is wise to stay away from alcohol.

MYTH: I am more careful when I drink, so it is OK to drive

Drinking and driving is extremely dangerous because alcohol slows reaction time, depth perception and judgment. In some parts of the world, where there is better monitoring and recording of accidents than in India, it has been shown that almost half of all fatal motor vehicle accidents are caused by alcohol.

MYTH: I can sober up quickly by drinking coffee

Drinking coffee or any other stimulant does not speed up ethanol metabolism. You may feel more awake, but the alcohol is still present in your body and therefore many functions are still impaired. Coffee can only help in limited ways and is not a sobering agent, and definitely not a license to drive drunk. One can consciously hydrate the day after drinking to recover better from the effects of a hangover, but no approach, no pill, no amount of coffee or tea, should make you think that you can operate heavy machinery or drive after drinking.

MYTH: If the government banned alcohol, there would be fewer alcohol-related problems

Unfortunately, history has taught us that this is not true either. Prohibition in the USA in the early twentieth century was a colossal disaster. Not only does prohibition, as exemplified by the current ban in many of the North East Indian states and Gujarat, fail to curtail the consumption of alcohol, but it also increases crime and causes a huge circulation of illegally-produced alcohol that is often very dangerous. Prohibition in India implemented by Morarji Desai in the Bombay presidency was directly responsible for the creation of the first Dons of the Bombay underworld because it handed them the control of the alcohol business instead of the licensed shops having control. Indirect prohibition on the poor caused by raising alcohol and molasses taxes fails to reduce the consumption of alcohol by the poor because it turns them to hooch seeking. Death tolls due to hooch consumption in late 2011 in West Bengal should be an eye opener to anyone wanting prohibition or maintaining increased taxation on alcohol. Prohibition and social taboos result in binge drinking in shoddy places, along with increased incidents of drunk driving. The best strategy to combat alcoholism is education, women empowerment, socio-economic equity, maintaining social and family bonds and strict enforcement of the illegality of drunk driving.

In large amounts, alcohol is a very dangerous drug that can and does cause death and destruction. However, in smaller doses alcohol can have a positive effect for a large segment of the population. So if you enjoy alcohol, enjoy it responsibly. Follow the Japanese concept of "haragei", or the old Indian concept of "madhyam marga" which encourages not filling yourself up to your throat with food or drink alike. So, if one must drink there are responsible ways of enjoying a drink or two. Moderate drinking is no more than 2 drinks for women and no more than 3 to 4 drinks for men in a day, preferably well spaced with snacks or meals to slow ethanol absorption. The benefits of drinking, however, can be outweighed by the risks when moderate-drinking turns to binging, and these dangers should offer sufficient warning to anyone binging to take the happy middle path of moderation or quit altogether.

MYTH: Occasional binge drinking does no harm

US National Institute on Alcohol Abuse and Alcoholism defines binge drinking as a pattern of drinking that brings a person's blood alcohol concentration above 0.08 percent. This usually takes around five drinks for males and four for females in a span of approximately two hours. A person does not need to measure his or her own blood alcohol level to know if he or she is binging; self-awareness and assessment of friends is usually sufficient. Binge drinking, especially as a regular pattern, is associated with many health problems including alcohol poisoning, liver diseases, cardiovascular diseases, sexual dysfunction and fetal alcohol syndrome in unborn children of a pregnant binger. In addition, according to the US Centers for Disease Control and Prevention, binge drinkers are more than 10 times more likely to report driving under the influence of alcohol compared to non-binge drinkers. While the correlation between alcohol and crime is undeniable, there is heated argument as to whether alcohol actually causes crime or merely acts as a societal permission slip for perpetrators to commit preconceived crimes, as suggested by some placebo alcohol studies. Without doubt, blackouts due to heavy inebriation leave people vulnerable to crimes of predation such as rape.

.

Chapter 2
What is causes deaths from drinking tainted alcohol in India?

Within many batches of hooch produced illegally reside substances that will provide drinkers with the kick that they are looking for but when contaminated, can also result in death. Such illicit alcohol related deaths are not commonplace in all parts of the world but a recurring occurrence in countries like India and Russia. Illicit liquor in India is frequently added with additional distilled alcohol and ammonium salt called "Nausader" in Hindi, to spike up the potency. If the additional distilled alcohol has methanol contamination, in significant amounts instead of it being pure ethanol, poor victims end up paying the price with their health and lives. Methanol can be produced in the distillation process of alcohol produced from sugars, if the distillation temperature is allowed to rise too high. Ethanol has many problems itself, but rarely causes mass deaths. The presence of methanol in hooch is usually unintended result of carelessness because the makers of the illicit alcohol will lose customers if it is known they produce tainted product. For industrial purposes, methanol is used in antifreezes, fuels, and solvents. It is also known as wood alcohol because in the past, it was produced almost exclusively as a byproduct of wood distillation. Methanol is difficult to distinguish from ethanol because it smells and tastes similar to ethanol, but is actually a little bit sweeter

The reasons this bad alcohol is continuing to be made, sold, and consumed is a large societal issue and will likely take months or years to sort out. However, if people know what this "hooch" is doing to their bodies and can recognize the symptoms recognize the fact that help is needed, hopefully many lives can be saved in the mean time.

Methyl alcohol or methanol is extremely toxic and can cause death in amounts as small as 30ml. When methanol enters the body, it can initially cause similar inebriation symptoms to ethanol-containing safe alcohol. In addition, one may become nauseous, experience vomiting, abdominal pain, and central nervous system depression, which could manifest as lowered body temperature, heart rate, or breathing rate. If you experience these symptoms it is best to seek professional heath care assistance. At this point methanol poisoning is very treatable.

After the initial inebriation, there is a period of 12-24 hours where it may seem like nothing is happening. Internally, the human body is metabolizing the methanol into formaldehyde and eventually formic acid. The increased acidity in the blood and other body tissues has many severe consequences. The mildest of these is temporary or permanent blindness. Eventually, respiratory failure and death can occur. Mortality rates strongly correlate to the length and severity of this increased level of acidity. Patients who survive may suffer from permanent neurological disorders and may resemble Parkinson's patients.

If methanol poisoning is identified early on (before high levels of acid are accumulated) the metabolism of methanol can be inhibited through the administration of ethanol. The same internal machinery that breaks down methanol will be used to break down the ethanol instead and the more toxic methanol will be excreted through the kidneys. If high levels of acid are already present in the blood health care professionals will need to purify the blood through hemodialysis or other methods.

In summary, if you experience nausea, vomiting, abdominal pain, a decrease in your heart rate or breathing, or blurriness or loss of vision after drinking hooch, you may have methanol poisoning. This is a potentially life threatening condition, but is treatable. Recognizing these symptoms and seeking help may save your life.

While economic realities and ill governance drives hooch production in India there are several factors that contribute to its devastating effects. You have read so far about the health and lack of education contributing to hooch tragedy but now we would like to focus on another systemic problem that exacerbates the devastation of Hooch. Law enforcement agencies are in some part and are perceived as bullies by poor people of India. While there are several good officers, for the have-nots the police atrocities cover the whole gamut from more common mild harassment of verbal bullying, and everyday corruption to even in some instances murder and rape. It is a common practice by police to deny filing a complaint and to fail to act even if the complaint is lodged. Poor people are afraid to seek police help or report a crime, leave alone go to them when they have actually broken the law. Drinking Hooch is breaking the law. The Dec 2011 hooch tragedy of West Bengal in which 171 people died is a glaring example of how fear of police contributed to increased death toll. First this tragedy could not have happened if the police force was not in the pockets of the local alcohol mafia. Secondly, and more importantly even when people started feeling the symptoms of methanol poisoning, shockingly they did not head to hospitals for the fear of police harassment. Sadly this was not the first instance of this nature and is unlikely going to be the last. We need to make police in India friendly and accountable to common man. Additionally even though the rules have changed "on paper", people still are afraid to take a stranger to the hospital for the fear of police harassment. Earlier physicians could not even start treating patients until a police report was filed. Hopefully the changes in law would soon manifest in form of cultural changes

Chapter 3
Is Prohibition the answer to alcohol woes of India?

Enjoying a couple drinks is not synonymous with the risky behavior of binge drinking. Nonetheless, binge drinking is a rising trend on college campuses, hostels, and amongst the neo-rich and illiterate sections in India. Given that healthy alcohol consumption and alcohol abuse are both rapidly increasing, especially with a burgeoning middle class, we need to tackle the good, the bad and the ugly of alcohol head on before it gets out of control.

In the last few years, there has been a dramatic rise in rehabilitation clinics and NGOs mostly professing prohibition. Many NGOs are asking for prohibition, increased taxation, retaining bans on alcohol products, and limiting sale outlets. Regardless of the intentions, it is obvious that their efforts have been at best ineffective and in most cases counterproductive. In addition, many genuine grass root movements of concerned citizens, especially the mothers and wives of addicts, have resulted in gaining sufficient momentum for a ban on alcohol to become a state and central election issue. Prohibition by late populist chief minister N. T. Rama Rao in Andhra Pradesh was a result of such a grass root movement founded in the socio-economic costs of alcohol abuse in the agricultural sector. The prohibition in Andhra however, was rather short-lived and an utter failure, much like the current bans in Gujarat and Mizoram. Banning the regulated sale of safe alcohol has resulted in people consuming hazardous alcohol of shoddy quality, binging in secrecy, and driving far distances to consume alcohol, which results in increased alcohol related traffic incidences. The bans have also meant the loss of much needed revenues for a growing India that regulated alcohol sales generate. This counterproductive nature of prohibition is a global trend and the American prohibition era and Pakistan's prohibition from the Zia era onwards are good case studies for anyone wanting to evaluate the merits and demerits of going dry.

Unfortunately, due to a lack of data acquisition, reporting, and monitoring by federal and state agencies, there is very little large-scale data available on drinking patterns in India. This deficiency of empirical evidence is debilitating for effective policy changes, but it is not the only bottleneck preventing a mature national debate on alcohol consumption. The main blockade is the immature political agenda that amounts to an unproductive and pretentious debate siding alcohol vs. no alcohol in black and white terms instead of shades of gray that change depending on the context The hundreds of deaths in Orissa and Gujarat due to illicit liquor should have been a wakeup call for the need to change this inflexible and infantile alcohol debate. Despite the glaring failure of prohibition, not just the government is to blame. Many anti-alcohol organizations have been unrelenting in their demands for prohibitory rules rather than encouraging healthy alcohol policies and education. Just like forcing abstinence is no way to solve the problem of sexually transmitted diseases, prohibiting alcohol is no way to cure the evils of alcohol addiction and binging. It is unlikely to expect that recently unveiled increases in the health budget and more donations to prohibitionist NGOs are going to fix the problem of alcohol abuse. Sales of alcohol, whether legal or illegal, will continue as they have in the past. What can make a difference though, is the spread of information on alcohol abuse. In a democracy, the buck really stops with the private citizen; hence this piece is intended as food for thought for drinkers and potential drinkers so they can make their own informed choices.

It is claimed by some federal reports that the epidemic of binge drinking can account up to 45% of total consumption in the US. Activists organizations against regulations put the numbers much lower, but still at shocking levels. The data for India is limited, but the trend is towards steep increases in binge drinking, as is the case in other economies where alcohol is a forbidden fruit – a societal taboo. Binge drinking has various definitions, but in general, consists of rapidly raising a person's blood alcohol concentration. This usually takes around 5 drinks for males and 4 for females in a span of approximately 2 hours.

Binge drinking, especially as a repeat pattern, is associated with many health problems including alcohol poisoning, liver sclerosis, cardiovascular diseases, sexual dysfunction, and fetal alcohol syndrome. In addition, according to the Center for Disease Control and Prevention (CDC) of the USA, binge drinkers are over 10 times more likely to report driving under the influence of alcohol compared to non-binge drinkers. The World Health Organization (WHO) estimates that 2.5 million deaths per year worldwide are caused by alcohol related incidents including drunk driving. A strong correlation also exists between alcohol and crime, though one can debate if alcohol actually causes crime or merely acts as a societal permission slip for perpetrators to commit preconceived crimes, as suggested by some placebo alcohol studies. Given the infestation of many cities with rapists and muggers, especially the National capital territory, accepting any drink from a stranger or binging in the presence of strangers should be a big no.

We may sound like we are using hypocritical scare tactics while criticizing prohibition, but hold on, remember we just talked about health benefits of alcohol in the first chapter. If you drink then all we are saying that you should make the time of sharaab a time for suroor and not a time for blackout and hangovers. Make it a social lubricant and not a societal burden. Alcohol should not be thought of as a forbidden fruit, as cultural taboos in contemporary India have made it out to be. It should not be a vehicle for teenage rebellion or an exit route from the rural life of a broken village and its traditions. Multiple studies on college drinking in the USA, Australia, and UK have shown that people overestimate how much their peers are drinking and hence binge due to peer pressure. Across multiple studies, the strategy of publishing college drinking habits actually has been shown to encourage more responsible drinking habits. Alcohol is not really that special on its own. It is only as special as the person enjoying it and the company that makes pleasant moments, lifelong memories and friendships.

Simple economic, age, gender and professional dimensions that define alcohol consumption patterns in small homogenous western nations are insufficient in a multilayered society like India. Despite adoption of western lifestyles, middle class in urban India has yet to entirely do away with the old mores and values. For few in the big city, the old values are still the core of their identity, while for others they are suitable pretenses, resulting in schizophrenic environment where youngsters grow up absorbing the worst of both the eastern and the western influences.

Rural India is witnessing a different yet equally seismic shift, where the old joint-family value system and associated economic enterprises are collapsing and people are moving away from traditional professions. There is significant migration in search of livelihood due to ever shrinking size of the agricultural land holdings. Apart from the stress of displacement, a break from ones communities also removes the social safety net that keeps check on alcohol abuse. In some previously semi-arid and moderately populated regions, improvements in irrigation and industrialization of agriculture has created excess wealth and removed the need for few previously agricultural people to work with their own hands. Instant money for these people and also for the land holders in areas near big cities where prices of real estate have sky rocketed has resulted in youngsters who do not know how to handle their newfound wealth and are prone to addiction.

Alcohol abuse combined with ready availability of opium derived drugs seeping in from our western borders has resulted in a whole generation of addicts in Punjab, Jammu, Haryana and parts of Rajasthan. In the flux of values and economic relations of our multilayered society four denominators are can still describe the major pillars of alcohol related problems in India: 1) lack of information 2) adulteration of alcohol 3) inefficient alcohol regulation policies and 4) the paucity of appropriate medical intervention.

While the debate over the merits of alcohol consumption is hotly contested worldwide, the views about alcohol consumption in India usually do not come in shades of gray but often in black and white. There is a taboo concerning alcohol consumption in any amount, especially by women and conservative sections of society, but also in general due to religious teachings of the Vaishnav sect of Sanatan Hinduism, Islam, Jainism, Sikhism, and Arya Samaj and the remnants of anti-alcohol Gandhian drive. Actual practice of alcohol consumption is altogether a different matter, which covers the whole gamut from healthy consumption to fatal abuse. History has taught us that making something a taboo does not solve the problem; it only makes the forbidden fruit more tempting. Taboos encourage closeted and unsafe behavior like binge drinking in the case of alcohol or unsafe sex in the case of premarital relationships. Humans have been enjoying alcoholic beverages since prehistoric times. Alcohol has been celebrated in the Vedic hymns, Shaivism, Buddhism, Tantra, streams of Catholicism, and many indigenous animist and tribal traditions that celebrate alcohol in moderation. In fact many anthropologists and biologists claim that it is likely that alcohol from fermented grains was used as food source much before the bread was invented. In fact, if consumed in moderate amounts over many years, alcohol can have numerous positive health consequences. Moderate amounts of alcohol have been correlated with reducing dementia and Alzheimer's disease, improving cardiac functioning, and reducing stroke incidences, type 2 diabetes, osteoporosis, gallbladder diseases, arthritis, renal cell carcinoma, thyroid cancer, and non-Hodgkin lymphoma among many other diseases.

When alcohol is consumed in an uncontrolled and excessive manner however, the story is much different. Binge drinking, especially as a repeat pattern, is associated with many health problems including alcohol poisoning, liver sclerosis, cardiovascular diseases, sexual dysfunction, and fetal alcohol syndrome in unborn children of pregnant women. The World Health Organization estimates that 2.5 million deaths per year worldwide are caused by alcohol related incidents, mostly due to heavy inebriation. A strong correlation exists between heavy alcohol consumption and crime. Also, heavy drinking can result in blackouts that leave people vulnerable to crimes such as rape. Apart from health issues, the economic drain and the disruption of societal peace due to increased crime can be quite a big strain on society. Heavy alcoholics (not mild healthy drinkers) are more often involved in domestic abuse than rest of the population. So instead of making something taboo we need to understand a drink or two a day is good for health, unless the woman consuming is pregnant or if someone is patient of a kidney or a liver disease. On the other hand heavy amounts, i.e. more than three to five drinks a day, depending on the size of person, not just causes health issues but it wrecks families. The solution is in moderation for those who like to drink and not in professing abstinence.

Apart from lack of information on alcohol for people to make their own informed choice, adulteration of alcohol and lack evidence based regulation policy are reason for grave alcohol related health problems. As we discussed before, most alcohol related poisoning is due to non-ethanol alcohols in badly produced hooch. In fact, most hooch related tragedies, like the recent one in Gujrat, have happened in dry states or on dry days in wet states. This is not surprising. When one cannot get regulated good quality alcohol and it is taboo to consume alcohol, people resort to shoddy alcohol consumption in hiding. Such prohibition on alcohol also results in binging due to fear of being caught. Failure of prohibition in Gujrat and Mizoram and earlier in Andhra should be an eye opener. This counterproductive nature of prohibition is a global trend and the disasters from the American prohibition era and Pakistani prohibition from the Zia time onwards should act as stern reminder for anyone professing prohibition. Well-intentioned grass roots movements due to lack of information frequently push for prohibition and so do the self-benefiting NGOs that are merely acting as fronts for converting black money to white through Hawala schemes. One needs a non-prohibitionist, informed grass root movement to set the minds of ruling political elite to focus on the problem of addiction and alcohol abuse in India.

We are also missing well-trained physicians with information on efficacy and availability of de-addiction drugs and an awareness of benefits of psychological, exercise and vocational therapies. Appropriate information to both the health professionals and the family of addicts can result in much needed counseling and support required for anyone wanting to quit alcohol addiction.

Just to reinforce what we have said we would focus on a specific example. Gujarat is one of the large states that implements prohibition on alcohol and makes for an interesting case study. Not many years ago, Gujarat's government made crimes relating to illicit liquor production and sale punishable by death, while continuing prohibition. On the other hand prohibition encourages illicit alcohol use and mafia growth associated with its trade. It is important to note that current government did not pass the prohibition law per se but has upheld the prohibition that is in place from the time of Morarji Desai. Technically, the state assembly has not and cannot pass separate laws that decide the extent of punishment for a crime at state level. Only the federal assemblies of Lok Sabha and Rajya sabha can make such changes to the constitution. What the state assembly actually did, was that it now asks prosecutors to press for murder charges and not criminal negligence for alcohol related deaths. At a cursory look, it appears to be a good step, as we can deeply sympathize with the logic that anyone who kills poor people, directly or indirectly, should be held accountable for manslaughter. Looking a bit closer, the reality is quite different. The implication of such law in the existing Indian legal system is that scapegoats and some poor end-executors of the offense and not the masterminds get the book thrown at them. If one looks at people who are booked under this law, there is no single fat cat facing the wrath of the book so far. Gujarat High Court, not to be left behind the legislative, recently urged a stricter implementation of prohibition, as if prohibition is the cure of the problem of alcoholism.

The use of prohibition and extreme punishment as a reaction to alcohol problem is not unique to India. Historically across the globe, a war has been waged on the name of fighting the evils of alcohol by employing heavy incarceration and death penalty. In the US, the prohibition era saw laws passed with heavy penalties for bootlegging. Interestingly, alcohol consumption went up during that era and so did the crimes associated with bootlegging. Worst of all, the bootlegging mafia was actually behind the imposition of prohibition and strong punishments associated with bootlegging. This mafia could get the law selectively imposed, as happens in Indian dry states now. The mafia controlled several politicians and both through violence and political connections eliminated the competition that would have existed in a fairer and freer market. This experience was not exclusive to America or to the Western hemisphere but has been and is currently true for many developing countries too.

Prohibition has been an utter failure in India too and having heavy penalties for bootlegging is at its best, an ill-conceived treatment of cultural symptoms and at its worst, tool for the mafia to expand their criminal activities. One only needs to follow the money trail to find who are drumming up support for prohibition in India and who funds the prohibition advocacy charities of Babas, Mullahs and Rajnetas in New Delhi and one would know the intentions. A brief look at Indian history would show you that it is not that different from the US experience. Morarji Desai's decision to ban alcohol in the Bombay Presidency in the early 50s was the chief cause of the growth of the smuggling syndicates and the likes of Haji Mastan, Vardarajan, Karim Lala etc., who were the founding fathers of the Mumbai underworld. This started the funding of the Godfathers who eventually bred the likes of the criminals who once temporarily dented the plural unity of India and with serial bomb blasts dimmed the spirit of Bombay.

In India another form of prohibition is extremely steep pricing of legal and safe alcohol. This comes in the form of heavy taxation, along with setting the price of ingredients such as molasses exorbitantly high. This is directly responsible for selective death of poor people. In the absence of safe affordable alcohol, poor people binge on unregulated alcohol or hooch. Whether this prohibition is a road to hell paved by good intentions or it is simply malicious conniving scheme by special interests is not obvious in all cases but what is obvious is that it is clearly it is a counter-productive approach. If we want to save lives, we need to keep safe alcohol legal, spread education on alcohol abuse and then implement a strong punishment for illicit alcohol trade that targets the owners of such operations and not the poor workers. Punishment for illicit alcohol, in the absence of safe alcohol does not work and only supports mafia.

In a simple-minded way, one may view the solution to make the poor people to simply quit drinking alcohol. Not that different from Sanjay Gandhi's infamous compulsory sterilization approach. We know that despite religious injunctions and governmental regulations, alcohol consumption has not decreased. We are not promoting alcohol use and would wish all its abuse went away, but we are making a case for what has proven to be effective – an evidence-based alcohol policy. Simply looking away or implementing a knuckleheaded and malicious prohibition would not solve the problem.

Apart from the price issues, let us briefly look at reasons why the economically backward stratum is especially vulnerable to the illicit alcohol consumption. Some of the reasons are true for the entire developing world, while some of the religious ones are more specific to India. First, alcohol offers a transient escape from the everyday grind of what may be quite rightly considered a very sorry existence. Consumers crave many substances of abuse when they are under emotional stress. Given that bad planning has resulted in uneven economic growth, the massive migration of young men away from their families creates an environment where men have minimal familial and societal bonds. Alcohol related crimes and abuses, especially domestic abuse, occur most often in places with poor gender equity. India, with its remnants of feudal mind-set, is consistently trailing more than 100 other countries when it comes to gender equality. Despite large-scale economic development, the mental and philosophical outlook of many Indians is sadly stuck in a past era. There is not an easy fix to that issue expect education and social mobility. Wide scale, holistic education and women empowerment are desperately needed to solve the problem. Another reason for alcohol abuse is that the current versions of almost all major religions in India make alcohol a taboo. This results in the consumption of alcohol in hiding, instead of moderate social consumption like that in Mediterranean European nations that embrace the positive aspects of alcohol. Prohibition, social taboos, a lack of education and lack of gender equity, poverty, and the outrageous pricing policy of alcohol that specifically targets poor people are all ingredients in the recipe for making a hooch tragedy. What is direly needed is to lift the heavy taxation that selectively targets poor, police abuse of the poor, and prohibition regulations. Equally direly needed are education, gender equity and economic empowerment of poor, so the need of single young people to migrate away from families and being involved in irresponsible is reduced.

In this book we have highlighted some counterproductive and hypocritical approaches. It would only be appropriate to end the book pointing at one of the most laughable and pretentious acts of alcohol regulation in India. There is currently a ban on alcohol advertisements while allowing alcohol manufacturers to advertise products like music CDs and bottled water that have the same name as their alcoholic beverage. All major alcoholic product manufacturers advertise ostensibly non-alcoholic products with the same name or similar named products, logos and overall appearances as their alcoholic products. Worse than that, most of the advertised products are actually nearly non-existent. In all the cases, the manufacturers are paying more for the advertisements of these proxy products in a month than the decades of sales of these proxy products.

It is a laughably travesty of law that should be amended with no delay. If as a society, we decide that it is acceptable to have alcohol advertisement in mass media then that is fine but what is the point of allowing such an openly exploited loophole? If we decide that there should be a continuation of ban on the advertisements of alcoholic products then the manufacturers should be forced to comply with having different visible logos and names of alcoholic and non-alcoholic products.

In summary, at all levels as a society we need to be more honest to ourselves and understand that alcohol regulation can indeed work if it is honest and in shades of gray. Prohibition does not work. We must work towards improvements in economic and social equity, education and health care instead of politicizing alcohol. An educated and well to do society is necessary for reducing alcohol woes, just as is availability of medical intervention and strict punishments for domestic violence, drunk driving. A smarter alcohol production and regulation policy that is based on hard data and proven strategies, instead of religious dictates, would help India benefit from alcohol and reduce the troubles because of alcohol addiction!

About Sukant

Dr. Sukant Khurana is a scientist, artist, writer, and entrepreneur. He was born in Delhi, India and has spent most of his professional career in United States. His science focuses on understanding functioning of brain, ameliorating human suffering through technology development, and data science, while his art focuses on exploring the human condition. Sukant has worked on efforts to encourage education, sustainable development, women empowerment, environmental, and healthcare issues. In free time, Sukant can be found working on various art projects, traveling off beat paths, capturing wildlife on his camera or having long chats with friends over a cup of coffee.

Photocredit: Costance Burkin

About Brooks

Dr. Brooks Robinson got his Ph.D in neuroscience from the University of Texas, Austin. He is currently researching opioid addiction at Oregon Health Science University. During his stay in Austin, Tx, he collaborated on both neuroscience research and science outreach with Dr. Khurana. Brooks is a big lover of adventure sports. In his free moments, he enjoys participating in athletic events or exploring outdoors.

Connect with Sukant

I really appreciate you reading our book! Here are my social media coordinates:

Facebook author and artist pages:
https://www.facebook.com/SukantKhuranaauthorsite https://www.facebook.com/Sukant-1625360857788363/

Twitter: https://twitter.com/sukant_khurana

LinkedIn: http://www.linkedin.com/pub/sukant-khurana/43/a23/755

Websites:
http://www.brainnart.com
http://www.dataisnotjustdata.com

Connect with Brooks

I really appreciate you reading our book and hope to hear from you about addiction issues. Here are my social media coordinates:

LinkedIn:
http://www.linkedin.com/profile/view?id=1236089 10

www.ingramcontent.com/pod-product-compliance
Lightning Source LLC
Chambersburg PA
CBHW061938280526
45787CB00004B/1648